A LEADER'S JOURNEY

Communication

By Mike T. Lightner

Chief Master Sergeant (Retired), US Air Force

D2D
DARE2DREAM
LEADERSHIP DEVELOPMENT

Alaska

Printed in the United States of America

First Printing, 2021

ISBN-13:
Paperback: 978-0-9996570-7-2
Hardcover: 978-0-9996570-8-9

Dare2Dream LD Productions
dare2dreamleadership@gmail.com

www.d2dleadership.com

TABLE OF CONTENTS

A LEADER'S JOURNEY

INTRODUCTION

If you had read my book Lead Bold – Lead Strong – Lead Well, then you know my story. Like the main character in this book, Bob, I was an energetic young leader, burning his way up the promotional ladder, way to focused on succeeding to see what was truly going on. I was frustrated, tired, overworked, underpaid, and often thought to myself "if I just work a little harder, things will get easier...things will get better...my time will come." The truth was...my time was coming but it wasn't the success I desired. It was the painful truth, the truth I hadn't even considered, the truth was...I was failing and didn't even know it.

Luck, fate, a blessing, call it whatever you like but right in that moment, at the very time in my life, when I needed it the most, I was introduced to a book that would transform my career and my life forever. This wasn't a big book, in fact it only has 111 pages, but it taught me about leadership in a way that connected with me like no other book could have at the time.

What is this all powerful, life changing book, the book that turned everything around for me? No, it wasn't the Bible. Although, that book is powerful and life changing as well. It just wasn't what I needed at the time and to be frank, I probably wouldn't have appreciated its true greatness.

The book I'm referring to is The One Minute Manager by Ken Blanchard and Spencer Johnson· It is a story book and shares the journey of a bright young man, who was wanting to learn more about becoming an effective manager· I was captivated by this book and couldn't set it down· I felt a connection to the young man and felt I too was on this journey with him· As he learned, I learned· As he became more successful, I took what he and I were learning, applied it in my own career, and I too became more successful·

This is why, when I became an author, I just knew I needed to write a book like this· A story book, with leadership principles embedded throughout· A book that could take the reader on a journey and start the reader on a new journey of their own·

Although the story in this book is largely a work of fiction, it starts out much like my own leadership journey, a young man, sitting in his office alone, doing everything he believes to be right, only to be confronted by someone who cared enough to say something and call him out on his misguided behavior.

I hope you will not only join Bob on his journey but will take what you have learned in these pages and set your own career and life on a new path as well.

To my brother Greggory A. Maske.

You lived your life on your

own terms, were your own boss,

and charted your own course.

I love and miss you!

ACKNOWLEDGMENTS

I have to say a huge thank you to all the marvelous minds whose work has contributed to my own growth over the years and consequently ended up in this book in different forms.

A LEADER'S JOURNEY

The Leader's Journey!

COMMUNICATION

THE LEADER

Bob was a Small Shop Chief, working in a company that inspected and maintained the safety and survival equipment on commercial airliners. This equipment included life preservers, oxygen masks, life rafts, escape slides and various other items required to keep the aircrew and passengers safe in the event of an inflight emergency. It was a demanding field, one that required perfection because just one little mistake, could cost someone their life.

Having worked for this company for several years, Bob was very good at what he did. His hard work, selfless service, and dedication had resulted in him being promoted, ahead of many of his peers, into the leadership position he now held. From Bob's perspective, he was a success and well on his way to bigger and better things...or so he thought.

OUR STORY BEGINS

Our story begins on what seemed to be an ordinary Friday. Bob was in his office, busily working on paperwork, while the rest of his team was across the hall taking care of the daily maintenance workload. Then, without warning, with a simple knock on the door, Bob's ordinary day came to a screeching halt.

As Bob opened the office door, he was surprised to see his Superintendent standing on the other side. From the look on Bob's face, he was clearly annoyed by the interruption, but he mustered up a smile and did his best to force out a warm greeting.

"Good morning Mr. Holt, to what do I owe the pleasure of your visit this morning?" Bob said.

Mr. Holt replied, "We are here to do a courtesy visit and spot inspection."

Bob had been through many of these courtesy visits and spot inspections in the past and saw them as little more than a waste of time.

Without really thinking through what he was saying, Bob replied, "Does it have to be now? I'm busy trying to get caught up on all this paperwork and don't really have the time for this."

Mr. Holt, clearly surprised by Bob's statement, smiled slightly and responded, "Yes Bob, we are going to do this now. If you don't feel you have the time to escort us around, just ask one of your people to do it and we will come see you when we are done."

Bob, still frustrated by the interruption, agreed, and walked Mr· Holt and his assistant across the hall to the maintenance area where the rest of his team was busily working·

Once there, Bob signaled for a young lady named Angela to come over to where he, Mr· Holt and his assistant were standing·

[Angela, known by most as Angie, was a lovely young woman from the south with a pleasing personality and deep burning desire for getting results. Because she was a professional working mother of two young kids, her husband John quit his job as an aircraft mechanic in order to stay home with the kids and save the cost of daycare. She was not happy about the interruption, but you would never know it by her pleasant attitude and beautiful smile.]

Once Angie had arrived where the three were standing, Bob said, "Angie, Mr· Holt and his assistant will be doing a courtesy visit and spot inspection· I would like for you to escort them around and answer any questions they may have·"

Angie warmly greeted the two visitors "Hello, it is a pleasure to see you both again· What would you like to see first?"

Upon hearing that, Bob turned and headed back to his office·

A couple hours later, Bob was interrupted again by a knock on the door. As he moved towards the door, he thought to himself...what now? I am never going to get all this paperwork done with all these interruptions!

Frustrated, Bob swung open the door and without thinking said "WHAT!"

To his surprise Mr. Holt and his assistant were standing there. A bit embarrassed by his less than professional greeting, Bob said, "Oh, Mr. Holt...I'm so sorry, I didn't realize it was you. Is there something I can help you with?"

WHAT WENT WRONG?

Mr. Holt responded, "Bob, we have seen all we need to see for now."

Hearing this Bob's mind started to wonder...what went wrong? I've been through many of these visits in the past and they were never this short. Someone must have screwed up...just give me a name and as soon as you leave, I'll fix them!

Mr. Holt went on, "We are going to stop our inspection for now and schedule a time to come back at some point in the future."

Bob, still wondering what could have gone wrong, stood there in silence hoping whatever the problem was, would soon be revealed to him. Little did he know, the next words he would hear would forever alter the course of his life and career.

Not one for mincing words Mr. Holt said "Bob, we get the impression, you are so far in over your head, that if you looked up, you couldn't see the light of day."

Bob stood in silence not knowing how to respond. In his head, he was appalled at the accusation. After all, he and his entire team were working their tails off...12-hours a day, and often times, 6-days a week. He thought...what are you talking about, with our budget, low staff and these untrained, unmotivated people you keep sending here, what do you expect? This is not my fault...this is not my fault!

The next few hours were a bit of a haze and before long, Bob found himself at home thinking back through the events of the day. And as much as Bob tried to push the blame for all his shop's problems on to others, he came to realize two things.

First was the acceptance of Mr. Holt's statement. Bob was in way over his head. His shop was stuck. Sure, they would start to make progress in one area, but then new problems would surface somewhere else. They would get someone trained and someone would leave. They were stuck alright, and Bob had no clue on how to get them unstuck.

The second thing Bob came to realize was, if he didn't change, they were going to change him. Meaning, if he didn't become the person who could fix the issues they were having, they would bring in someone else who could.

Bob spent the rest of the weekend thinking through his situation and trying to figure a way out.

Then, Sunday night, as he laid his head on the pillow, Bob knew what he needed to do...he needed to swallow his pride and ask Mr. Holt for help.

SETTING PRIDE ASIDE

As Monday morning rolled around, Bob found himself standing outside of Mr. Holt's office. Still not sure of what he was going to say, he sat quietly hoping the right words would come to him.

Without warning, the silence was broken as Mr. Holt's assistant said "Bob...Bob, Mr. Holt will see you now."

Bob slowly got up and made his way into the office. Feeling a bit defeated and embarrassed, he walked in with his head hung low, looking a little like someone who had just lost their favorite dog.

"Good Morning Mr· Holt," Bob said·

"Good Morning Bob, how can I help you?" replied Mr· Holt·

"That's just it," responded Bob, "I'm not really sure how you can help me but it's clear to me now, I do need some help·"

"Wonderful, Bob," said Mr. Holt with a smile, "recognizing we need help is the first step we need to take in getting the help we need. How about you tell me what's been going on over there and we will put together a plan for how we are going to equip you to turn things around."

Hearing this, Bob began sharing all the challenges he had been faced with over the past couple of years. The lack of funding, inadequate manpower, poor training, and sheer overload of paperwork were just a few of the many things Bob brought up, but more importantly, was the problem he was having with moral and frequent miscommunications he was having with his staff.

When Bob was done, Mr. Holt thought for a few seconds and then said, "Bob, how about we start by focusing on the communication problems and then we will move to the others, sound good?"

THE STUDENT IS READY

Feeling a bit defeated, at this point, Bob was willing to try anything, so he said, "Sure, if you think that is the best place to start."

"Great!" exclaimed Mr. Holt, "why don't you tell me a little about each of your team members?"

"OK, I guess we could start with Angie," responded Bob, "she is a hard charger and moves quickly to get things done. Not as old or as seasoned as some of my other team members but what she lacks in experience, she makes up for in confidence and decisiveness. All of which, I think are great, but there are days it seems like all she wants to do is argue, and on those days, I think she believes she is the one in charge."

After hearing this, Mr. Holt said, "Think back to the last time you asked for her opinion on something. Do you recall her saying something like 'I think we should' or 'I feel like we should'?"

Hearing this, Bob started to laugh slightly and said, "That's easy, she is always saying 'I think we should' this or that. She never seems to have any problem sharing her thoughts. In fact, the only problem is that sometimes she shares her thoughts too often."

"OK, when you give her a project to do, does she ask a lot of questions or just take whatever information you give her and run with it," Mr. Holt asked.

"She definitely takes it and runs with it," responded Bob, "In fact, half the time, she gets going so fast, I have to reel her back in because she took off without having all of the information or took the project off in a totally different direction than was expected."

Bob thought for a second and then went on to say, "Next, there is Paula."

[Paula is a middle-aged woman full of life and energy. She is also a working mom with two school aged kids and is married to Tony, who is an accountant. Paula loves to be with people and most people seem to like to be around her.]

Pausing for another brief moment before continuing. "Half the time, I can't tell if she comes to work to socialize or actually work. She talks all day and I mean all day...about anything and everything. In fact, if no one else is around, she just talks to herself. This actually makes her very good at speaking with customers but can cause some issues with her actually getting any work done in the shop."

"And how is Paula when it comes to projects," asked Mr. Holt, "does she ask a lot of questions or does she tend to run with it?"

"Oh, Paula asks questions." answered Bob "But they don't really seem to have anything to do with the project I've given her. Normally, her questions have to do with the people she can work with on the project. In fact, many times she will come back to me about project details because she forgot what I had told her or didn't hear something during our conversation."

"Ok, who else do you have on your team Bob?" asked Mr. Holt

"Well, there is Donna," said Bob

[Donna is slightly older than Paula and also has two adult kids. Her first husband had passed away from cancer a few years ago but she has since remarried to Joe who is disabled and medically retired from the military.]

"She is a little quiet but is very loyal and gets her work done," continued Bob "Donna doesn't deal with change or conflict very well. In fact, it seems like she does everything she can to avoid them. She is great at remembering people's birthdays and helping to set up shop get-togethers but once the event gets going, she tends to just stick around the people she already knows from work."

"Bob," Mr. Holt asked, "I think you know what my next question is going to be, but I'll go ahead and ask it anyway. How is she when it comes to projects?"

Bob thought for a few seconds and said, "Unlike the other two, she seems to really listen to what I'm saying. She often writes things down and asks questions about things I said that she wasn't clear on. The biggest problem I have with her is that she seems unsure of her own thoughts and ideas. Instead, when something doesn't go just right, she will come back to me and ask what she should do."

"Ok Bob, I think we have time for just one more," said Mr· Holt, "who else do you have over there that you would like to talk about?"

"Just one more, Terri," said Bob, then he thought for a few seconds·

[Terri is a bright young woman in her early 30s. She also has two school age kids and is single. Her kids' father was killed in a motorcycle accident, so she works hard to support herself and her kids.]

"Terri... she confuses me. She is always on time for work and her work is always perfect. The problem is, she is so detailed it makes her so much slower in getting things done. Don't get me wrong, I like things done perfectly but we have a lot of work to do, so we need both perfection and speed. And before you ask, when it comes to giving her projects...she will sit there and take all kinds of detailed notes, ask for things like examples and references, and ask question after question after question. And the most frustrating thing is, she takes forever to make a decision on anything. In fact, if she isn't one hundred percent sure...she won't make a decision at all."

"Bob, there is a tool I learned when I was a young leader that I think can help you," said Mr. Holt, "would you be willing to take the time to learn it and commit to trying it out over the next few weeks?"

Bob quickly responded, "if it will help keep me from getting fired or replaced, I'd be willing to try just about anything."

They both smiled.

Mr. Holt continued "Great! The name of the tool I will be teaching you is called the Maxwell Method of DISC. It is a process of identifying other people's personality styles and then speaking to them in a way that is more in line with the way they prefer to be communicated with. There are online DISC Personality Indicator reports available for purchase at maxwell-disc.com but for what we are going to do here, I don't think you need to get those for your folks just yet. Instead, I'm going to teach you some questions you can ask and some things you can look for to help you determine what personality types you are currently working with. Sound good?"

"Sounds great!" Bob enthusiastically replied.

JUST THE BASICS

"*Perfect!*" exclaimed Mr. Holt, "*To start with you need to understand that our personality and behavior are shaped primarily by three main things; heredity, our environment, and our role models. Heredity is basically who we are set to be from birth. This is the part of us that is pre-programmed in our DNA. Our environment will impact our style as well. In fact, life experiences, especially emotionally charged ones in our developmental years, can have a big impact on our personality style. Lastly, there are role models in our lives who teach us what is valuable, or who may even reward us for certain behaviors in order to reinforce those behaviors within us. Each of these three factors contribute to the makeup of who we are! Any questions so far?*"

"Not yet," answered Bob.

"This is important," continued Mr. Holt, "because two of the three of these may change over time or based on a sudden emotional life event and that will more than likely impact a person's personality. Because of this, as leaders, we must be equipped with the knowledge to know where a person's personality is, at any given time. This enables us to adjust our communication approach based on what will work best for them. Are you still with me Bob?"

"Yes, but I do have one question. What does DISC stand for?" Bob asked.

"Great question, each letter in the name DISC stands for one of the four basic personality styles." Replied Mr. Holt "The "D" stands for Direct or Decisive and measures how a person is likely to solve problems or responds to challenges. The "I" stands for Inspiring or Influencing and measures how someone attempts to influence or persuade the people around them. The "S" stands for Steady or Stable and measures how a person is to undertake activities or responsibilities. And, the "C" stands for Cautious or Compliant and measures how a person will normally respond to rules and regulations."

Bob looked down at his notes and stated "Let me make sure I got this right, D's are Direct or Decisive, I's are Inspiring or Influencing, S's are Steady or Stable, and C's are Cautions or Compliant, is that correct?"

"You got it, Bob," said Mr. Holt. He then got up from his desk, walked over to the printer, pulled out a blank piece of paper, sat back down and drew a large square divided into four smaller squares. At the top of the large square he wrote the word "outgoing" and at the bottom he wrote "Reserved". Then on the left side of the large square he wrote "Task Oriented" and off to the right he wrote "People Oriented".

After completing this, he looked up at Bob, who was paying close attention to what he was writing, and said "Bob, up here in the upper left corner is where we find our "D" or Dominant type people."

As he wrote a letter "D" in the upper left small square, Mr. Holt continued, "The people tend to be more outgoing and task oriented. They are very direct, competitive and care about results. Their greatest fear is being taken advantage of."

Mr. Holt then moved the tip of his pen over to the upper right square and put a letter "I" and said, "Over here next to them are our "I" type people, they are our Influencers and tend to be outgoing and people oriented. They are enthusiastic, friendly, and Optimistic. Their greatest fear is being rejected."

Bob sat there in silence watching as Mr. Holt moved his pen to the lower right box and said, "Down here on the lower right we find our "S" type Steady people. They tend to be more reserved and people oriented. They are sincere, patient, and modest. Their greatest fear is loss of security."

As he moved his pen to the lower left square, Mr. Holt continued "In the lower left, we find our "C" or compliant type people. They tend to be task oriented and reserved. They are accurate, cautious, and organized. And their greatest fear is criticism.""

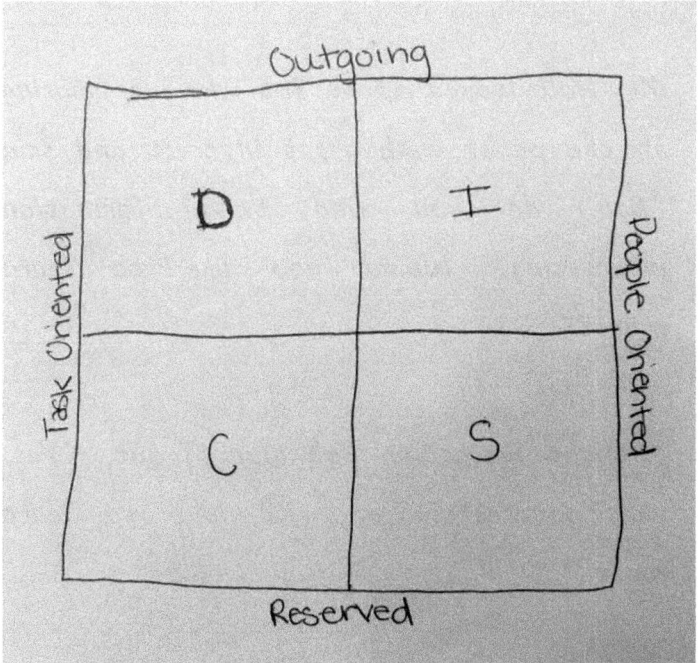

Mr. Holt looked up at Bob who was staring at the paper with great interest and said "Bob, do you find this information interesting? Would you like to learn more?"

Without hesitation Bob blurted out, "Yes, very interesting and I'd love to learn more."

Hearing this, Mr. Holt smiled and replied, "Great, over the next few weeks we are going to spend some time working with each one of these and you're going to go back and apply what you're learning with each of the four folks we discussed earlier. Sound good?"

Bob shook his head up and down while saying, "Yes, sounds good".

Then, Mr. Holt added, "Now, it is important to remember, we are all a blend of all four of these personality styles. So, you may see a little of all of them in each of your team members. But for what we are doing here, we are going to focus on their dominant style or the one that stands out the most. To help you with this, I'm going to send you back to your office with a worksheet I received during a Maxwell DISC Leadership course I had attended with Dare2Dream Leadership Development. This worksheet has really helped me to figure out other people's DISC style from normal everyday interactions with them and I think it will help you too.

As Mr. Holt handed the worksheet to Bob, he continued, "I want you to go back to your office, make four copies of this worksheet and put the name of one of the folks we discussed early at the top of each sheet. Then, over the next few days, every time you talk with one of them, I want you to go back to your office and start to document the behaviors that you observed."

Observed Behavior			
seems impatient	is talkative	seems nice	asks a lot of questions
asks about results	focuses on the experience	asks about the process	wants facts and data
seems bored with details	is willing to talk to others about it	wants to know who would be affected	wants to hear about the steps involved
has a serious and direct tone	shows their emotion	has a supportive tone	has a serious and questioning tone
seems to want control	seems to want excitement	seems to want to minimize change	is focused on it being perfect
seems to be competitive	easily shares information	is friendly	is observant
seems serious	seems adventurous	seems calm	seems reserved
is very direct	keeps the conversation light	makes me feel good	listens carefully
seems very important	seems very popular	seems relaxed	seems to be analyzing the information I am sharing
Total X's	Total X's	Total X's	Total X's
D	**I**	**S**	**C**

(For a copy of the Observed Behavior worksheet visit http://www.maxwell-disc.com/)

"Ok," Bob said with a slight hesitation.

Mr. Holt, sensing Bob's hesitation, said, "Bob, it isn't that hard and trust me...you will get the hang of it fairly quickly. Remember to make four copies of it because you will need one for each of them. I'll see you here in my office at 7:30 A.M. Monday morning Bob and we will be focusing on Angie next week, so do your best to get her worksheet all filled in as much as you can."

Bob said, "I sure will!" then turned and left Mr. Holt's office.

OBSERVED BEHAVIOR

As soon as Bob arrived back at his office, he went directly to the copy machine and made four copies of the Maxwell Method of DISC Observed Behaviors worksheet that Mr. Holt had given him. He then put Angie's, Paula's, Donna's, and Terri's names on them, put them each in their own folder and placed them on his desk.

No sooner had Bob set the folders down and Angie walked into his office, clearly upset about something.

As Angie plopped down in the chair, Bob asked, "What's up Angie?"

Without hesitation, Angie responded "What is wrong with these people? I ask them to do things as part of that project you assigned me but they don't seem to be taking the tasks seriously. Just this morning, I asked Donna for a progress update and she gave me some bull about needing more time because she had to do something with her kids last week and couldn't get to the project. Then, when I asked Terri how she was doing, she responded with more questions than I could count. It would have been faster for me to just do this myself!"

Thinking back on his conversation with Mr. Holt earlier that morning, Bob wasn't really sure how to respond, so he simply said, "Let me look into it and I'll get back to you."

By the frustrated look on her face, this was clearly not the answer Angie was looking for, but she nodded her head, stood up, and quickly exited the office.

As soon as she left the office, Bob pulled out the worksheet with her name on it and started going down the list.

"Let's see," he thought to himself as he read, "did she seem impatient, talkative, nice or ask a lot of questions? Impatient, definitely impatient." So, he placed an X next to the seems impatient block.

"That wasn't so hard," he thought, "Next row, did she talk about results, experience, process, or data? Another easy one. She was definitely worried about everyone else's lack of results."

Bob looked at the next row and thought to himself "did she seem board with details, want to talk to others about it, interested in who would be affected, or want to hear about the steps in the process?"

Bob reflected back on his conversation and then told himself "I don't think I have seen or heard enough about this one to answer it. I should skip it and move on to the next."

And so Bob went down the rest of the worksheet placing Xs in the behaviors he had observed and skipping the ones he had not.

When he was done, Bob looked over the sheet and noticed he had been able to put six Xs on the paper and all of them were in the D column.

Happy with his initial progress, Bob thought to himself "it is starting to look like Angie might be a D. That does make sense because she does always seem to be outgoing and task oriented. I better fill out more of the worksheet just to be sure."

A few minutes later, Paula walked into the office and sat down· "Good Morning Boss, how is your day going?"

Without giving Bob time to respond, Paula went on to say "you got to have a talk with Angie· She is out of control...showed up at my workstation this morning yammering on about some project she was working and something I was supposed to be doing to help her with it· I honestly don't remember her saying anything to me about it and besides, if she had, there still seems to be lots of time before it's due· I don't know what her issue is· She needs to lighten up, just because we are at work doesn't mean we can't have some fun and she is like a fun sucker· She walks in the room and boom, all the fun is sucked right out· Am I right? Isn't there something you can do?"

Bob, trying to get a word out, finally raised his hand as if signaling for Paula to stop talking. Then he said "Listen Paula, I'll talk with Angie but if she asked you to do something on the project, you need to get it done and not wait until the last minute like you have in the past."

Paula quickly responded, "Ok Bob, no need for you to get on me about this too. I'll get with her and see what it was that she supposedly asked me to do and when she needs it done. Man, everyone is so serious around here these days. No one seems interested in just having a good old fashion conversation."

And with that, Paula got up and left the office.

Bob pulled out the worksheet with Paula's name on it and then started going down the list. "Let's see" he thought "defiantly is talkative, was also very concerned about everyone's experience at work being fun, was defiantly willing to talk to others about it, was very friendly, and did seem to want to keep the conversation light. That is four checks in the I column and one in the S column for Paula. She is starting to look like she might be an I but I better keep working on her sheet as well."

Bob, closed the folder and laid it back on the stack with the other ones.

A few hours later, after returning from lunch, Bob arrived back in his office to find Donna sitting there quietly waiting on him·

"Hello Bob, did you have a good lunch" she said, greeting him as he walked through the door·

"Yes, I sure did" responded Bob "is there something I can help you with?"

Donna, slowly and in a somewhat of a quiet voice said "well, now that you mention it, there is. I'm a little worried about Angie and Paula. They just don't seem to be able to get along. Just this morning I heard them arguing over a project Angie has been working on and it seems like Paula either forgot about it or was procrastinating on it."

Bob nodded his head up and down, as to acknowledge what she was saying.

"Now, I don't want to get in the middle of all this" Donna continued "but their arguing is a bit disruptive to the rest of us. Besides, everyone knows how unpredictable Paula can be, she has never been good at details and I don't understand why Angie would expect her to be any different on this project."

Bob continued nodding his head and this time let out a verbal "aha" as if to signal for her to continue with what she was saying.

Donna went on "Speaking of Angie, she is out of control when it comes to this project. I know she asked me to take care of a few pieces of it and I will get them done but my family and the other members of this shop are way more important to me. In fact, recently I had to take one of my kids to an appointment and couldn't get something done as quickly as Angie wanted and she went off on me. She really hurt my feelings and it seemed like the more I tried to get her to calm down, the more upset she got. I know we are not supposed to bring our feelings to work and it's just business and all that other stuff but she really hurt my feelings and I can't just pretend that didn't happen."

Then Donna looked up and noticed Bob was actually listening to her, unlike previous conversations when he would be doing three other things while she talked, he was fully engaged in what she was saying and for once she felt like he had truly heard her. Pleased with this shift in Bob's response, she said "thank you so much Bob for taking the time to listen to me. It really means a lot to me."

Bob responded "you're very welcome Donna. Thank you for bringing this to me, I'll be sure to look into it and have a talk with Angie but I'll be sure not to mention your name when I do."

Comforted by this and Bob's promises to keep her name out of it, Donna got up and walked out of the office.

As soon as Bob was sure she was gone, he reached over and pulled out the Maxwell DISC Observed Behavior worksheet with Donna's name on it and started to go down the list.

"Let's see" he thought to himself "She didn't seem impatient, she was a bit talkative for a change, she seemed very nice but she is always very nice, and she didn't ask a lot of questions. I think the best place for the "X" is in the seems nice block."

With this thought, Bob put an "X" in the seems nice block and continued on with the worksheet. When he was done, he looked at the sheet and noticed he had put Xs next to seems nice, has supportive tone, is friendly, seems calm, makes me feel good, and seems relaxed.

Then he thought to himself "wow, it really seems like Donna is going to come out of this as an S. I guess I shouldn't be surprised by that, she has always been so supportive of others and really seems to just want everyone to get along."

Happy with the progress he was making, he put the folder with her worksheet back on the pile and thought to himself "wow, Donna is right, that was a much different conversation than we normally have. I actually enjoyed that and I feel like it was so much more effective for the both of us. I think from now on, when someone comes in to talk or ask a question, I'm going to make sure I set everything aside and pay closer attention to what they are saying and how they are saying it."

As the end of the day approached, Bob realized the only person he hadn't talked with and started filling in their worksheet was Terri, so he called over to her workstation and asked her to come over to his office.

As Terri approached Bob's office, he could see she looked a bit nervous. When she arrived at the open doorway, she stopped as if to wait for permission to enter and said "Hello, Bob. You called and requested to see me?"

Bob said "yes, thank you for coming over so quickly. I've talked to everyone else today about the project I had asked Angie to work on and realized I hadn't heard from you. How do you think it is going?"

Terri thought for a few seconds and said "Bob, I know you're busy and I don't want to disrupt all of the important work you do but I have a lot of questions and Angie doesn't seem willing or able to answer any of them. Because of this, I'm not really sure what I should be doing or how I can possibly be expected to do anything to help."

"Ok, what kind of question do you have?" Bob responded.

Without much hesitation, Terri went on to ask question after question about the project...the objective...timeline...budget...etc... and Bob did his best to answer as many of them as he could.

Then Bob said "Ok Terri, I think that is enough for now. Why don't you type up the rest of the questions you have and I'll get with Angie and see if we can't get you some answers?"

Happy with the prospect of getting her questions answered, Terri smiled and responded, "sure, I'd be happy to do that." She then got up and started to walk out of the room, but before leaving she said "Bob, thank you."

Bob just looked at her with a puzzled look on his face as if to say "for what?"

But before he could say anything, she added "thank you for taking the time to listen to all my questions and for trying to answer as many of them as you can. I know I ask a lot of questions sometimes and I just want you to know how much I appreciate you making the extra effort."

After hearing this Bob responded, "you are very welcome, I'm happy to do it."

As Terri left the office, Bob thought back on his previous conversations with Terri and how different they had been· He even felt a bit embarrassed as he realized he had rarely taken the time in the past to listen to her questions, let alone try to answer them· He then reached for the stack of folders and pulled out the Maxwell DISC Observable Behaviors worksheet with Terri's name on it·

As Bob thought back on the conversation, he had just had with her, he smiled a little as he read asks a lot of questions and he thought to himself "yep, that is for sure. No one asks questions like Terri does." He then went down the rest of the worksheet placing Xs next to wants facts and data, wants to hear about the steps involved, has a serious and questioning tone, is focused on it being perfect, is observant, seems reserved, listens carefully, and seems to be analyzing the information I am sharing.

Seeing this, Bob thought to himself "wow, clearly Terri has a C type personality. But I should probably speak with her again and fill in a few more blocks." He then put her worksheet back in its folder and placed it with the others.

As Bob turned back to his computer and what he had been working on, he noticed the time and thought "Time to go home already, where has the day gone?" He then packed up his things and headed for his car and the long drive home.

Over the next four days, Bob made a focused effort to talk to each of the four team members a few more times. Each time, he would go back to their Maxwell DISC Observed Behavior worksheet and review what he had marked and fill in some of the blanks. However, just before it was time to go home on Friday afternoon, Bob noticed something he hadn't expected to see. For some reason, the team members all seemed to be in better moods and getting along. He even had to admit to himself that this was one of the best weeks of work he had experienced in a long time.

As he packed up to head home for the weekend, Bob grabbed the folders with the worksheets in them so that he would have them for his Monday morning meeting with Mr. Holt.

NEW HOPE

Bob was so excited to talk with Mr. Holt and share with him the information that he collected, he could hardly sleep on Sunday night. When his alarm finally went off, Bob hopped out of bed, took a quick shower and headed downstairs for a quick breakfast.

Bob's mood was light and he felt like a kid again. Even his wife noticed the extra spring in his step and commented "well, you sure seem eager to get to work this morning."

With a smile on his face, Bob responded "you know what, I am. I'm actually excited to be going to work and seeing Mr. Holt this morning. I honestly would have never dreamed of saying something like that but I'm truly excited to be learning about this Maxwell Method of DISC system he is teaching me."

As Bob went to rush out the door, he went over and kissed his wife on the cheek, something he use to do when they first got married but somehow had just gotten out of the habit of doing the past few years. She smiled and said "well...I don't know what this DISC thing is but I'm already a fan of the impact it is having on you."

As Bob was driving to Mr. Holts office, he thought about his wife's statement and the things that had been happening over the past week. Then, he said to himself "she is right, I do seem to be enjoying my work again and I didn't feel nearly as stressed this weekend as I had over the past couple of years."

When Bob arrived at Mr. Holt's office, he was already seated at a small conference room table with a cup of coffee and some papers.

"Come on in Bob" said Mr. Holt, gesturing towards an empty chair on the opposite side of the table. "have a seat and show me what you were able to come up with on the worksheets you filled out on your team."

Bob sat down and before Mr. Holt could say anything else, he said "Mr. Holt, I really appreciate you taking the time to share the Maxwell Method of DISC with me. I know last time we talked, you said we would just be focusing on Angie this week but would it be possible for us to work on them all instead?"

Mr. Hold smiled and said "Bob, I'm a little surprised by the request. Last week when we talked, you looked like I was asking you to sell one of your kids and today you're wanting me to throw you into the deep end of the pool, headfirst."

They both laughed a little and then Bob said "True, this time last week, I honestly didn't see how me spending time on something like this was going to help me or my team get out of the hole we are in· However, after meeting with my team members last week, in an attempt to fill out these worksheets, I've already started to see some positive changes in the way we communicate and work together· And if all that is possible from filling out a worksheet, I'm super excited to see what will happen when we actually start using the rest of what you have to teach me·"

In a lighthearted laughing voice, Mr. Holt commented "That is wonderful Bob. Now, let's take a look at those worksheets."

Opening the top folder, Bob said "The first one is on Angie. As you can see, the results show her as a D but I'm not really sure I remember what that means or why it is important for me to know it."

"Bob" said Mr. Holt "As I recall, Angie was the young lady you asked to show us around when we were out visiting your shop and it doesn't surprise me at all to hear you say you believe she is a D. In fact, I pegged her as a D as well."

With that said, Mr. Holt dug through his papers and pulled out one that said Maxwell Method of DISC Styles Of Communication. He then said "Bob, I'm going to send you back with some information I received from Dare2Dream Leadership Development during that Maxwell Method of DISC Leadership course I had taken. This was the same course I was telling you about last week when I gave you the Observed Behavior worksheet."

THE PLATINUM RULE

Bob nodded his head, acknowledging he remembered him mentioning it.

Then, Mr. Holt asked, "Have you ever heard of 'The Golden Rule?'"

Bob nodded as if to say yes and said "Sure, treat other people as you would like to be treated."

"That's right Bob" replied Mr. Holt "The problem with 'The Golden Rule' is it assumes other people want to be treated like you like to be treated and the reality is, they probably don't. With the Maxwell Method of DISC, we learn how to treat and communicate with other people in the way they like to be treated based on their personality style. The folks at Dare2Dream call this 'The Platinum Rule' and I think you will soon see why."

Bob leaned forward, eager to learn more about this 'Platinum Rule' and how it could help him help his team.

"Today we will focus on how to communicate better with each of the four personality styles· Then, I will work with you and help you develop a communication strategy for each of the four people you have filled out worksheets for· Sound good Bob?"

Bob with excitement on his face and an eagerness to get started blurted out "Absolutely!"

——— *The* MAXWELL METHOD ———
DISC STYLES OF COMMUNICATION

If you are communicating with someone who demonstrates these CHARACTERISTICS	THEY MAY BE A	Consider using this COMMUNICATION APPROACH
» Confident » Assertive or aggressive » Challenges the status quo » Seems to like control » Dislikes routine	D	• Be direct and brief. • Stay in the big picture. • Don't try and share all of the details. • For a decision, provide them with options. • Maintain your focus on results, not process.
» Talkative » Optimistic » Encourages others » Fun to be around » Very social	I	• Allow them the opportunity to share their ideas. • Keep the conversation fun. • Don't overwhelm them with too much data. • Expect to follow up with them. • Provide short, concise information in a friendly way.
» Loyal » Reliable » Good listener » Avoids confrontation » Mediator	S	• Keep the conversational tone pleasant and friendly. • Steer clear of confrontational words or attitude. • Express your appreciation for their dedication and loyalty. • Focus on maintaining a supportive tone. • Provide them with time to adjust to changes.
» Analytical » Organized and structured » Works well with a schedule » Prefers to work alone » Quiet and reserved	C	• Focus on facts. • Keep the tone professional. • Give them all of the details. • Provide them with time to analyze options for decisions. • Remember they may ask many questions because they process by gathering more facts.

The JOHN MAXWELL **Team**

(For a copy of the DISC Styles of Communication visit
http://www.maxwell-disc.com/)

Mr. Holt, very happy to see Bob's enthusiastic response, smiled, pointed to the part of the handout where it listed the characteristics of the D style personality type and said "As a D, you have probably notice that Angie is confident, assertive or aggressive, challenges the status quo, seems to like control, and dislikes routine...correct?"

Bob smiled and commented in a laughing tone, "among other things, yes."

"Perfect" Mr. Holt responded "then from now on, when talking with her you're going to" now pointing at the Consider using this Communication Approach section of the handout "be direct and brief, stay in the big picture, don't try and share all of the details, provide her with options for decisions, and maintain your focus on results...not process. Do you see that Bob?"

"Sure, I see that." replied Bob "but could you give me an example of what that would look like?"

"Ok, let's say I'm you and your Angie and I want you to take on a project for the shop." responded Mr· Holt "What I would say is something like this· 'Hello Angie, I'm going to put you in charge of xyz project, you can either ask some of the team to help you or you can do it by yourself but ultimately you are responsible for getting it done· I want weekly progress checks, where you will be expected to brief me on your progress· The process you use is up to you as long as the end result is etc...' Does that help Bob?"

Bob nodded his head yes and added "yes, believe I got it. It will take some getting used to but I will give it a try."

"Great" responded Mr. Holt "let's take a look at the next team member."

Bob put Angie's worksheet away and pulled out Paula's. He then said "Paula came up as an I, which based on what you told me about I's last week, I really wasn't all that surprised to see."

Mr. Holt smiled again and said "See how easy this is Bob, you're already starting to figure out the personality styles of other people simply by thinking about or observing their behaviors. In the case of Paula, it sounds like you've noticed she is talkative, optimistic, encourages others, fun to be around, and very social...correct?"

Bob said "yes" and nodded agreeably.

"Alrighty, so as it says here on the handout." Responded Mr. Holt while now pointing at the I area of the Consider using this Communication Approach section "when communicating with Paula you want to allow her the opportunity to share her ideas, keep the conversation fun, don't overwhelm her with too much data, expect to follow up with her, and provide short, concise information in a friendly way."

Bob, having heard this and looking at the handout thought for a few seconds and then said "ok, so if you were Paula and I wanted you to work on a project, I would say something like "Hello Paula, how are you doing today. We have this xyz project that needs to be done and I could really use your creativity in getting it done. This should be fun and I would expect we will need to talk frequently about your progress. I will send you an email with all of the details to include some deadlines that will need to be meet. Let's both set aside 10-minutes each day to talk and let's be sure to add that to our calendar, so we don't forget.""

"WOW, Bob" said Mr. Holt "you are really getting the hang of this. Following up with the details in an email is an excellent idea as I's can often times forget the details. I also love the idea of the 10-minute daily meetings because when working with I's, five 10-minute meetings are often times much more productive than one 50-minute meeting. There are just two things I'd recommend you consider. The first is, if you ask Paula 'how are you doing?' you give her as much time as she needs to answer your question. Cutting her off this early in the conversation could derail what it is you are trying to accomplish. Second, make an effort to smile as much as you can during your conversation. It may feel a bit unnatural at first but I think you will see it is worth it by the way Paula responds.

Satisfied Bob understood what he had said and ready to move on, Mr· Holt said "Ok, let's take a look at the next person's worksheet·"

Bob put away Paula's worksheet, pulled out the one on Donna and said "I have to admit, I was a little surprised on this next one· Donna can seem like the nicest person and then out of the blue, just explode· Sometimes bring up things from months ago...things we didn't even know she was upset about·"

"Ok, Bob" injected Mr. Holt "let me take a look at her worksheet and I'll see if I can help you understand her a little better."

Looking at the worksheet, Mr. Holt smiled and then said "Oh, Donna is an S. Our wonderful S's are the peacemakers. They just want everyone to get along and don't like to create waves. Because of this, if they don't feel safe expressing their thoughts or opinions, they will hold them in until they just can't anymore and then they let it all come out."

Chuckling a little at his last statement, Mr· Holt went on to say "with our S's it is important to remember, how we say something...our tone and speed...is just as important as the words we choose· So, as it says here on the handout, you want to keep the conversational tone pleasant and friendly, steer clear of confrontational words, mind your attitude, express your appreciation for their dedication, focus on maintaining a supportive tone and provide them with time to adjust to changes·"

"In fact, if I were to ask Donna to do something" Mr. Holt went on "it would sound like this 'Donna, thank you for taking the time to come see me today. I really appreciate you and all the hard work you do for us. You are really the glue that holds this entire team together. I also wanted you to know, Angie is working on a big project and as a result, we are probably going to all be asked to make some changes around here. I know you are comfortable with the way things are now, but I would like you to think about how much better off we will all be once we get in the habit of doing things a little different.'"

Hearing this, Bob said "WOW, I can really see how she would respond better to that." Then he laughed a little and said "I can also see how, if I were to talk to Angie like that, she would laugh at me and walk out of my office."

Laughing with Bob, Mr. Holt responded "that is right Bob. Ds and Ss are natural opposites and they would both respond poorly if you communicated with them using the other personality style's approach. Just remember, with Angie keep it short and to the point, and with Donna, take your time and speak softly. As an S, you can expect Donna will be loyal, reliable, and a good listener. She will also try to avoid confrontation and may try to act as a mediator if she senses any tension."

Bob put away Donna's worksheet, pulled out Terri's and said "OK, I got it. Let's talk about Terri before we run out of time."

Mr. Holt slid Terri's worksheet over to where he could read it and said "So, Terri is a C, a wonderful wonderful C. Bob, you may have noticed but I have a high I personally style. Because of this, I have really come to appreciate the skills and abilities C's naturally bring to the world. In fact, one of the major reasons I selected my current assistant is because she is a C."

"Interesting" Bob said with a curious look on his face.

Mr. Holt continued "You see Bob, like Ds and Ss the Is and Cs are opposites. This means, if they can learn to communicate and work together, they can really form a powerful team. This is because one person's natural strengths can make up for the others natural weakness, but that is a lesson for another day."

Mr. Holt smiled and winked at Bob and went on to say "today we are looking at communication. As you have probably already notice, our C's are analytical, organized, structured and work well with a schedule. They prefer to work alone, are quiet and reserved."

Bob smiled and laughed as he said "Yep, that is Terri to the tee."

Mr. Holt continued "As it says on this handout, when talking with Terri, you want to focus on facts, keep the tone professional, give her all of the details, provide her with time to analyze options for decisions, and remember she may ask many questions because she processes by gathering more facts."

Bob thought for a few seconds and said "OK, so if I were to ask Terri to do something, it would sound like this 'Terri, there is something I would like for you to take care of because I know you will give it the time and precision needed for it to be done correctly. As of right now, this is what I know'"

After listing out all the details, Bob Continued 'there may be a few things I'm missing and I would appreciate it if you could fill in those details as you work through the project. We are on a bit of a time crunch, so do your best to research this as quickly and as thoroughly as you can, given the limited time. I'll put some time on my calendar every Tuesday and Thursday from 3 to 4 pm for you to come and ask me whatever questions you may have. Are there any questions I could answer for you right now?'"

"That is wonderful Bob. You are really getting the hang of this." Said Mr. Holt "Just make sure you have enough time set aside to answer a few questions. If you run out of time, you could add something like 'I'm sorry Terri but we are out of time. Could you email me the rest of your questions and I'll do my best to have the answer before we meet about this again?'"

"OK, that is good advice. Thank you, I will" responded Bob.

Seeing that his time was up, Bob put Terri's worksheet away and put the Maxwell Method of DISC Styles Of Communication handout on top of the folders.

While Mr. Holt walked Bob to the door, Bob said "Mr. Holt, I really appreciate you taking the time to teach me this. I'm looking forward to getting back to the shop and trying out what I've learned."

Mr. Holt smiled and said, "My pleasure Bob, this has been fun for me as well."

STUDENT TO TEACHER

When Bob arrived back at his office, he was surprised to find Angie, Paula, Donna, and Terri waiting there for him·

After setting down his bag and coffee, Bob said with a smile "to what to I owe the pleasure of your company this morning?"

Angie was the first to speak out "Bob, we were talking and we have all notice you have been acting very strangely lately and we want to know what is going on."

Then Paula quickly followed "Bob, what Angie means to say is; we understand you are under a lot of pressure and we just want to make sure you are ok."

Bob, looked at Donna and Terri wondering which one of them would be next but they both just sat there with a concern look on their faces, nodding in agreement with what Paula had said.

As Bob sat their looking at his team in silence, Angie blurted out "come-on Bob, spill the beans...what is going on with you?"

In that moment, Bob decided it was time to let his team in on what was going on. Remembering what he had learned about how to best communicate with his team, Bob smiled and then talked slowly and softly but with confidence and purpose as he asked. "Do you all remember when Mr. Holt and his assistant came to take a look at our shop a little while back?"

They all nodded in agreement.

Bob continued. "well things didn't go very well for us that day and Mr. Holt decided he should end his visit early and focus on what he believed was the major issue...me."

They all just stared at Bob in disbelief of what he had just said.

"In fact" Bob went on "before leaving Mr. Holt confronted me about the fact that I was failing you and the organization and I didn't want to believe it. I kept telling myself it wasn't true. He was wrong and didn't know what he was talking about. I came up with an entire list of other things it could be like lack of training, personnel, equipment, funding and the list went on and on but the more I thought about it...the more I considered what was really going on here...I came to the realization, he was right."

Bob took a sip of his coffee before continuing. "We were stuck, and I had no idea on how to get us unstuck. So, I set aside my pride and went to Mr. Holt and asked him for some help. Something I probably should have done months ago. And, with his help, I've been trying to change the way I interact with each of you."

Angie, Paula, Donna, and Terri continued to listen, leaning forward in their chairs with interest.

"You see" said Bob "In the past, I have tried very hard to treat you all the same. You know, like the 'Golden Rule' says, 'treat other people how you want to be treated'. Well come to find out, that was a big mistake. Each of you are different...different from me and different from each other. Mr. Holt has helped me to see that using a system to help me to identify each of your personality styles called the Maxwell Method of DISC. Let me show you what I've learned so far."

Bob pulled out the individual Observed Behavior worksheets he had filled in for each of them and the Maxwell Method of DISC Styles Of Communication handout Mr. Holt just given him. He then looked at Angie and said "Angie, do you remember when we talked last week?"

Angie nodded and said "yes, in fact, that is when I first notice you were talking to me differently. I can't put my finger on just what was different, but I remember feeling like the conversation had gone so much better than any of our previous discussions."

Bob smiled and said "that is good, then I must have been doing something right. You see, after our first conversation, I started to fill out this observed behavior worksheet to see if I couldn't figure out your personality style. Not surprisingly, you were one of the easier ones to figure out."

Bob showed Angie the observed behavior worksheet he had filled out on her and then laid the Maxwell Method of DISC Styles Of Communication handout on top of it. He then pointed at the D row and said "Angie, I pegged you as a D...D's are Direct and Decisive, they are confident, assertive, challenge the status quo, seem to like control, and dislikes routine. Do you agree? Does that sound like you?"

Angie nodded and said "oh yes, especially the parts about liking to be in control and disliking routines...ugh...I really dislike routines. Especially, when they are not getting us any results."

Sarcastically, Paula blurted out "direct and assertive...who would have ever guessed?" Everyone laughed, even Angie

Sliding his finger over to the Communication Approach column of the D row, Bob went on to say "Angie, in the future, when we talk you can expect me to be more direct and brief, stay in the big picture of things, not try and share all of the details, provide you with some options, be more focused on results, and not get to much in the weeds on the process. How does that sound?"

Angie got a big smile on her face and replayed "that would be wonderful, especially the part about focusing on results. I do like to get me some results."

Everyone smiled and laughed

Bob then looked at Paula and showed her the Observed Behavior worksheet he had filled out on her, saying with a smile "Paula, you were fairly easy to figure out as well."

Now pointing at the I row of the Maxwell Method of DISC Styles Of Communication handout, Bob Continued "from what I've noticed you tend to be more like an I. I's are Inspiring or Influencing and tend to be talkative, optimistic, encouraging, fun, and very social."

Angie looked at Terri and said with a smile "talkative...really really talkative."

Paula put on her best serious face and said "what, I have a lot of important things to say" then, not being able to hold it back anymore, burst out in laughter.

Everyone laughed as Bob pointed at the Communication Approach column of the I row and continued "when we talk, I'm going to try to allow you the opportunity to share your ideas, keep the conversation fun, not overwhelm you with too much data at one time, follow up with you both verbally and in writing and provide short, concise information in a friendly way. Does that sound good to you Paula?"

Paula nodded with a smile and said "oh yes, that sounds wonderful Bob, especially the parts about keeping it fun and letting me share my ideas."

Bob smiled and said with a light laughter in his voice "good to hear, just know when we talk, I'll be setting a timer. So we will need to try to stay focused for the first few minutes of the conversation."

Hearing this, everyone chuckled

Bob then pulled out Donna's observed behavior worksheet and showed it to her, saying in a soft calm voice "Donna, you were a little harder for me to figure out but in the end you came out to have an S type personality. The S's are Steady or Stable and tend to be loyal, reliable, and good listeners. They also try to avoid confrontation and act as mediators."

Pleased with the way Bob was talking with her and with what she was hearing, Donna smiled and continued to listen.

Bob, pointed at the Communication Approach column of the S row and softly and calmly continued "when speaking with you, I will try to keep the conversational tone pleasant and friendly, steer clear of confrontational words or attitude, express my appreciation for your dedication and loyalty. I will also try to focus on maintaining a supportive tone and provide you with time to adjust to changes when I can. How do you feel about that?"

Donna's eyes light up as she smiled. She then answered "Bob, that would be just wonderful. I do like to feel like I am appreciated and don't like confrontation at all."

Bob responded "great, in fact, I think I speak for everyone when I say, we all appreciate you always remembering our Birthdays and the way you check up on us when you believe we are having a bad day."

Everyone looked at Donna and nodded in agreement.

Sensing Donna's discomfort with the attention she was getting, Bob showed Terri her observed behavior worksheet and said in a soft voice "Terri, you were the hardest person for me to figure out. Not because you are a bad person but because you and I are so different."

Terri smiled and said in a soft questioning voice "different?"

Bob said "yes, different. We are interested in very different things. Then, after going over your worksheet several times, I finally came to the conclusion that you have C type personality. The "C" stands for Cautious or Compliant. They are analytical, organized, and structured. They work well with a schedule, are quiet and prefer to work alone. What do you think about that Terri?"

Terri thought for a few seconds but before she could respond Paula spoke up and said "analytical, organized, and structured...yep that is Terri."

Everyone laughed and then Terri said with a look of complete sincerity "anything worth doing, is worth doing correctly the first time."

"That is right" said Bob "being correct is very important and you do a very good job of making sure we are all doing our jobs correctly. From now on, when I'm speaking with you, I'm going to try to focus on facts, keep the tone professional, give you all of the details, and provide you with time to analyze options for decisions. I'll also remember you may ask many questions because I now know you process information by gathering more facts. What do you think about that?"

Terri thought for a few seconds and said "I'm not really sure what to think yet, I need to read up on this Maxwell Method of DISC and learn a little more, then I'll get back to you."

Bob smiled and said "of course you do and of course you will, I'd expect nothing less than a thorough review from you before you provide me with your opinion. Thank you."

Bob then looked at his team members and said "I'm so glad that we were able to talk this morning and that I was able to share with you what I've been learning. I think this is going to be a new beginning for us as we stop using the 'Golden Rule' and start using the 'Platinum Rule.'"

With a look of confusion on her face, Paula said "'Platinum Rule'? Did I miss something...what is the 'Platinum Rule?'"

"Great question Paula" responded Bob "The 'Platinum Rule' is 'treat other people as they want to be treated' and now that we all know the Maxwell Method of DISC, we can all start treating each other in a way that the person we are communicating with, will be better able to process and receive. Ok...back to work."

Everyone smiled. They then got up and went across the hall to their workstations.

A NEW BEGINNING

Over the next few weeks, Bob continued to meet with Mr. Holt. He would then go back to his office and share with his team what he had learned. The more they learned, the more changes they made in their work center. Bob eventually appointed Angie as the lead project manager, assigned Paula as the customer relations point of contact and Donna was put in charge of training and daily operations. Bob then put Terri in charge of quality control.

Now, assigned positions in alignment with their natural strengths, each member thrived, shop morale was never higher, productivity went up, and the team started winning awards in product quality, timeliness of delivery and customer service. Even Bob himself was recognized as the Small Shop Chief of the Year but all this is a story for another day.

PUT IT INTO ACTION

The Maxwell Method of DISC takes the best of the Maxwell Methods of Leadership and Communication, which are built on the principles of leadership expert John C. Maxwell, and using a DISC based Assessment tool, provides you and your organization with something that is uniquely available through this program.

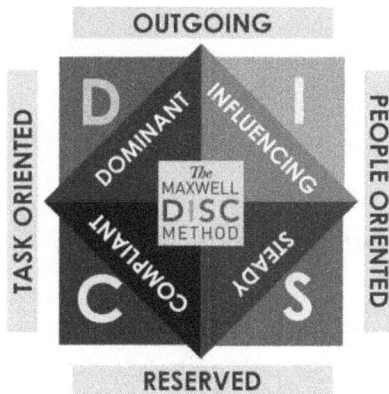

Visit www.Maxwell-DISC.com to start your assessment today.

If you're leading a D like Angie

Their Greatest Needs are:

- *Control, Being seen as competent, Admired*

To Motivate them:

- *Be brief and talk in terms of big picture.*

Create opportunities for them to be in charge.

- *Encourage them to help you make decisions.*

They are annoyed by:

- *People who are weak*

- *People who are indecisive*

- *Lack of leadership*

If you're leading a I like Paula

Their Greatest Needs are:

- Fun, Excitement, Approval, Encouragement

To Motivate them:

- Recognize their good behavior.

- Give them and opportunity to express their thoughts.

- Give them the opportunity for social time.

They are annoyed by:

- Boredom, Routine

- Being ignored

- Demands of organizations

If you're leading a S like Donna

Their Greatest Needs are:

- Peace, Stability, Appreciation

To Motivate them:

- Create a close relationship.

- Emphasize your need for their help.

- Thank them for their helpfulness.

They are annoyed by:

- Intimidation, disloyalty

- Unrest, malic, injustice

- Insincerity, conflicts

If you're leading a C like Terri

Their Greatest Needs are:

-    Perfection,   Sensitivity,   Continual reassurance

To Motivate them:

- Explain reasons for a desired action.

- Allow questions and suggestions.

- Give them an opportunity to research.

They are annoyed by:

- Inaccuracy, incompetence

- Disorganization

- Overly simplified explanations

THE END!

"I'm a success today because I had a friend who believed in me and I didn't have the heart to let him down."
~ Abraham Lincoln

Thank you for investing in yourself, buying this book and reading it! If you would like to find out more about some of our other learning resources, go to:

www·d2dleadership·com

SPECIAL THANKS!

I would like to say THANK YOU to some special people who really helped me with this book:

Angie Lightner

Lisa Hoffman

Joyce Lightner

Terri Lightner

Hannah Lightner

ABOUT THE AUTHOR

"When you truly believe in yourself and what you are trying to accomplish, others will believe in you and your vision as well."

~ Mike T. Lightner

Mike Lightner is a retired Chief Master Sergeant from the United States Air Force with extensive knowledge and experience in team leadership and personnel development. In his last position, as the Aircrew Flight Equipment Career Field Manager, he oversaw the leadership, growth, development and management of over

5,200 Total Force (Active Duty, Air National Guard, and Reserve Airmen, and civilian employees) worldwide. Additional, Mike was responsible for the inspection, maintenance, acquisition, and sustainment of over $8 Billion in critical life sustaining aircrew and passenger safety, survival, and chemical defense equipment.

As a John C. Maxwell Certified International Coach, Teacher, and Speaker, Mike offers workshops, seminars, keynote speaking, and coaching, designed to aid you in your personal and professional growth through study and practical application of proven leadership methods.

Mike's passion is to develop leaders who, in turn, have a passion to develop leaders. If this is the type culture you would like to create within your organization, he stands ready to help you achieve your goal!

mikelightner@d2dleadership·com

www·d2dleadership·com

www·maxwell-disc·com

OTHER BOOKS BY MIKE

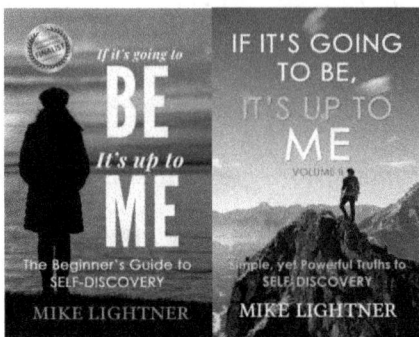

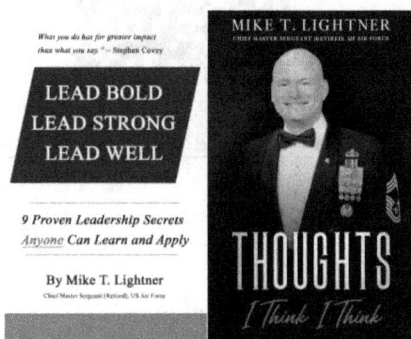

Available on:

Amazon

Barnes & Noble